FAMILY COOK BOOK

BY KERRYANN DUNLOP

PENGUIN BOOKS

HI GUYS, JAMIE HERE!

I'm really proud to introduce you to the illustrious Kerryann Dunlop. As one of my ex-students at Fifteen, I've had the pleasure of cooking beside Kerryann for many years now, and boy this girl can cook. Since her stint at Fifteen, she's honed her cooking skills, had a family, become a super-mum, and now she's got this beautiful book of 50 signature dishes from her busy household. As a mum on a tight budget, Kerryann's recipes are all about food that'll make you feel like you've had a big old hug, from comforting dinners and easy breakfasts to clever batch-cooking and naughty treats.

This little book is one of the first in a collection of no-nonsense, beautiful cookbooks, inspired by the incredible cooks, chefs and artisans on my Food Tube channel. If you don't know the channel already, hunt us out on YouTube, where myself and a bunch of super-talented people, including Kerryann, are uploading exclusive videos every week, with plenty of clever tips, tricks and methods that'll transform your cooking. We're a community of food lovers and experts, who simply want to share our passion with you guys, so if you have any questions, please leave a comment and we'll be happy to answer.

Kerryann is such a friendly character with a tone and style that are super-warm, motherly and gentle – so armed with the recipes in this book and the thrifty family tips and tricks from her Food Tube videos, you're guaranteed a bunch of homely recipes that you'll keep going back to time and again. That's enough from me, over to the wonderful Kerryann.

Big love,

youtube.com/jamieoliver

HELLO, I'M
KERRYANN

I've always loved cooking. Ever since I was little, I'd watch any kind of cooking programme on TV (Delia was always my favourite!) and when Food Network started, it was like Christmas. I'd always be in the kitchen, looking at what my Mum and Nan were cooking, and it's from them that I learnt how to cook. I grew up on good home-cooked food and it was my Mum and Nan who showed me that it's more than possible to make good food on a tight budget. Money's a big thing (I'm not rich!), but people are under the illusion that to eat well you need lots of it. You don't – you just need to be clever about how you shop and how you cook.

A lot of the recipes in this book are versions of my Mum's and Nan's, who passed down their knowledge to me. Since having kids, my cooking has become much more family-orientated – I don't want to feed them ready-meals and processed food, I want to feed them like my Mum fed me.

Even if you think you can't cook, it's not that difficult to learn – once you've got five recipes down, you're good. After that, you'll have the confidence to play around with those five recipes and make them your own, then who knows what you'll make next (my **hidden vegetable pasta sauce** on page 78 is my favourite – I use that sauce in so many recipes, from chilli and lasagne to pizza and meatballs).

I hope that you find your five recipes somewhere in this book, then you can do exactly what I did and make them your own.

Good luck and happy cooking!

DEDICATED TO . . .
Mr Jolly – this one's for you matey! xx
For Cory-Jay and Aliyah – the best things I ever made. xx

* * * CONTENTS

BREAKFASTS

SNACKS & QUICK FIXES

BATCH COOKING

DINNER TIME

SIDES

MY FIFTEEN STORY

When I got accepted onto Jamie's Fifteen Apprentice Programme all those years ago, my life changed forever, and I can honestly say it's been a home from home ever since. When I was sixteen, I went to chef's school, but it closed down halfway through my course and I ended up disheartened and disappointed by the whole idea – I thought my career as a chef just wasn't meant to be. Then one day, I got an application letter to sign up for the first year of Jamie's Fifteen programme and I filled it out immediately. We had to go through loads of rounds of interviews and I still remember having to taste test Jamie's butternut squash tortellini as part of that process and telling him I thought it was bland! To be fair, I was suffering from bronchitis at the time and I'd lost my sense of taste. I probably didn't make the best first impression!

When I was lucky enough to be selected, it was really daunting. I wasn't the best behaved apprentice and I don't think I'd have got away with a lot of things if I was on the course now, but Jamie saw something in me that I didn't. I just thought I was a good cook, but he had total faith in me. I remember at the end of one of the shows we did for *Jamie's Kitchen* on Channel 4, he said, "Kerryann will be a chef, I don't care what anyone says", and for that I'll love him forever.

Since leaving Fifteen, I've worked as a chef all over the place – as a pastry chef for Baker and Spice, in gastro pubs and now at a brilliant children's nursery, but the Fifteen family has stayed there with me all along the way. Even though it's been 11 years since I was first an apprentice, the team have supported me through thick and thin and I know I'll never ever experience that same support anywhere else. If it wasn't for Fifteen and for Jamie seeing my potential, I wouldn't have Food Tube and I wouldn't have had the chance to create this beautiful book, so for that, I'll always be grateful.

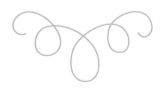

To find out more about Fifteen and the Apprentice Programme, go to:
jamieoliver.com/the-fifteen-apprentice-programme

MY TIPS FOR
MAKING FOOD FUN

• • • GET THE KIDS INVOLVED • • •

Ask your kids to help you make the dinner – get them to taste and mix ingredients and pick any herbs. The more they're involved in the whole process, the more they'll enjoy the food that ends up on their plates.

Take them shopping (I know it can be stressful!) and give them their own list of ingredients to look for. My kids get excited when they see that the food they helped to buy has ended up on their plates. If you can, take them to different farmers' markets too – get them to ask for ingredients and, if possible, let them taste different bits and pieces. It'll give them a better understanding of where food comes from too.

Kids also like to get the table ready and help to serve food. My kids love setting the table and pretending it's a café – they'll get out the salt and pepper, lay out the napkins and assign everyone a place. I'll sometimes bring the bowl or pan to the table and get them to share it out between everyone. I cook at a nursery school and the children there get really excited when I ask them to help out too.

SIT DOWN TO EAT AS A FAMILY

Eating with your kids and talking to them about their day is great – they see that you're willing to eat what they're eating and it's sociable. Rather than focussing on what they like or don't like, they're distracted and talking, and most importantly, they're enjoying it too.

JUST TRY IT

This is the only rule in my house. I never force my kids to eat anything, as long as they just have a go first. If they don't like it, then that's fine – they can leave it and try it again another time. When they were babies, I'd give my kids foods that I didn't like – if you don't like something, let your children have it anyway so they don't develop the same bad habits or dislikes that you have.

GET CREATIVE

Play around with ingredients and get the kids to do it too – buy purple carrots or turn plain mash green by stirring wilted spinach through it. The only time my son will eat coleslaw is if I make it with red cabbage, instead of white, then he loves it because it's so colourful! When he was younger, he hated broccoli, but I experimented with purple sprouting types and his opinion totally changed. The more fun you can make it, the more likely they are to give it a try.

Smoothies are a brilliant way to get creative – I've got a couple of recipes on pages 24–25, but I also like to let my kids have their own say on what they want to add – they love choosing their own flavour combinations and it's a great recipe that they can make from start to finish. Plus, you can't go far wrong with a smoothie so you can give them real ownership of it without worrying about the results!

BREAKFAST

Cereal simply doesn't cut the mustard in my house.

DIPPY EGGS & ASPARAGUS SOLDIERS

SERVES
4

TOTAL TIME: 15 MINUTES

1 bunch of asparagus (300g)

4 large free-range eggs

TO SERVE

sea salt and freshly ground
black pepper

optional: crusty bread

Place a large griddle pan over a high heat. Snap the woody ends off the asparagus, then add to the pan in an even layer and cook for 3 to 5 minutes, or until tender, turning occasionally.

Meanwhile, put the eggs into a medium pan, cover with cold water and place over a high heat. Bring to the boil, then reduce the heat to low and simmer for about 3 minutes for runny eggs. Meanwhile, get your egg cups ready – dippy eggs will wait for no one once they're done! Using a slotted spoon, carefully remove the eggs and place in the cups, then tap each shell gently with a teaspoon and remove the tops. Serve straight away, with the griddled asparagus for dipping, salt and pepper on the side and bread to mop up, if you like.

When it comes to dippy eggs, there are plenty of tasty treats you can dunk – try grilled chipolatas or **homemade fish fingers** (see page 86), which my kids love – I know it sounds odd, but it really works!

PANCAKES & BERRY COMPOTE

• • • SERVES 4 • • •

TOTAL TIME: 25 MINUTES

FOR THE PANCAKES

40g unsalted butter

2 large free-range eggs

180g plain flour

220ml whole milk

1 teaspoon baking powder

1 pinch of sea salt

FOR THE BERRY COMPOTE

1 vanilla pod or 1 teaspoon
vanilla extract

500g fresh or frozen mixed berries

3 tablespoons caster sugar
or runny honey

optional: 2 tablespoons
fresh unsweetened apple juice

To make the compote, halve the vanilla pod lengthways (if using), and scrape out the seeds. Put the pod and seeds, or the vanilla extract, into a medium pan with the rest of the compote ingredients (if you don't have apple juice, add 2 tablespoons of water instead). Simmer over a medium-low heat for around 20 minutes, or until the berries are soft and the liquid has reduced to a syrupy consistency, stirring occasionally.

Meanwhile, melt 25g of butter in a pan over a low heat. Separate the egg yolks from the whites, then place the yolks in a large bowl with the flour, milk, baking powder and salt. Whisk until smooth and thick with no lumps, then stir in the melted butter. In a separate bowl, whisk the egg whites into stiff peaks, then gently fold into the batter.

Melt a little butter in a heavy-based non-stick frying pan over a medium-high heat, then scoop spoonfuls of the batter into the pan – this'll make coaster-sized pancakes, but you can add more or less batter depending on how big you like them. Cook for 1 to 2 minutes, or until air bubbles start to pop on the surface, then flip over and cook until nice and golden on both sides. Stack the pancakes up on a plate and cover with a tea towel to stop them going cold (in my house, they're eaten too quickly to go cold!), then repeat with the remaining batter, adding a little more butter to the pan each time. Serve with the berry compote or your favourite toppings – I also like sliced bananas and honey.

This compote will keep for about a week in an airtight jar in the fridge – it's also good with Greek yoghurt and **granola** (see page 32), stirred through porridge or rice pudding, or even spread on toast like jam.

TOASTED BACON SANDWICHES
WITH FRIED TOMATOES

• • • • • •

SERVES 2

TOTAL TIME: 15 MINUTES

4 thick rashers of higher-welfare
smoked or unsmoked bacon

2 ripe tomatoes

olive oil

4 thick slices of crusty bread

freshly ground white pepper

Preheat the grill to high. Place the bacon on a baking tray and pop it under the grill for 3 to 5 minutes on each side, depending on how you like your bacon (I like mine nice and crispy round the edges). Meanwhile, cut each tomato into four thick slices. Place them in a frying pan over a low heat with a little oil and fry for 2 to 3 minutes on each side, or until warmed through and lightly golden. Toast the bread to your liking while the tomatoes are cooking.

Divide the bacon and tomato between two slices of toasted bread, season with a generous pinch of pepper (I love white pepper, but black is fine here too), pop the remaining slices of bread on top and serve straight away with a good cup of tea.

Swap the bread for English muffins here if you fancy a change. This recipe is really easy to scale up if you're feeding more people, and just as easy to halve if you ever find yourself home alone.

CHEESY SCRAMBLED EGGS

SERVES
2

TOTAL TIME: 10 MINUTES

olive oil

6 large free-range eggs

sea salt and freshly ground
black pepper

50g Cheddar cheese

TO SERVE

4 thick slices of crusty bread

Place a non-stick frying pan over a low heat to warm up and add a drizzle of oil. Beat the eggs with a little salt and pepper and pour into the frying pan. Stir continuously with a wooden spoon for about 3 minutes, or until the eggs are nice and silky and just starting to set. Don't get impatient and turn the heat up – this will make the eggs cook too quickly and they'll become rubbery and not very nice at all. Grate the cheese and gently stir it through the eggs until it starts to melt, then serve straight away on hot toast.

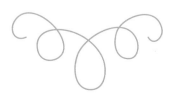

STRAWBERRY & BANANA SMOOTHIE

SERVES
2

TOTAL TIME: 5 MINUTES

Peel **2 medium ripe bananas** and trim **15 ripe strawberries**, then place into a blender with **2 tablespoons of Greek yoghurt** and **175ml of fresh unsweetened apple juice**. Whiz until smooth and thick, then have a taste and add **runny honey** to sweeten – the amount you'll need will vary depending on the ripeness and sweetness of the fruit. Pour into glasses and serve straight away.

MANGO & PINEAPPLE SMOOTHIE

SERVES 2

TOTAL TIME: 15 MINUTES

Peel ½ **a pineapple** and remove the core – it's tough and fibrous so would make your smoothie stringy – then dice the flesh. Peel and destone **1 large ripe mango** and place into a blender with the pineapple, **175ml of fresh unsweetened pineapple or apple juice** and the juice from ½ **a lime.** Whiz until smooth and thick, then have a taste and add **runny honey** to sweeten – the amount you'll need will vary depending on the ripeness and sweetness of the fruit. Pour into glasses and serve straight away.

SWEET EGGY BREAD

SERVES 6

TOTAL TIME: 20 MINUTES

6 large free-range eggs

75ml evaporated milk

sunflower oil

6 thick slices of white bread

2 ripe bananas, peeled

6 heaped tablespoons
natural yoghurt

runny honey

Whisk the eggs and evaporated milk together until well combined. Heat 1 tablespoon of oil in a large non-stick frying pan over a medium heat. Dip 2 slices of bread into the eggy mixture until well coated, shake off the excess, then add to the pan and fry for 2 to 3 minutes on each side, or until golden and crisp. Halve the eggy bread diagonally, then serve straight away with sliced bananas, a dollop of yoghurt and a drizzle of honey. Repeat with the remaining slices of bread, serving as and when they're ready.

You can make eggy bread into a savoury breakfast by ditching the bananas, yoghurt and honey, and serving it with crispy smoked streaky bacon and a drizzle of maple syrup instead. Add a dollop of ketchup on the side and it's heaven!

CORNMEAL PORRIDGE

SERVES
6

1 x 400g tin of light coconut milk

150g fine cornmeal

100ml condensed milk

¼ teaspoon ground cinnamon

1 teaspoon vanilla extract

1 pinch of sea salt

1 whole nutmeg, for grating

TO SERVE

runny honey

Pour the coconut milk into a heavy-based non-stick pan over a high heat. Fill the empty tin 1½ times with water and pour it into the pan, then bring to the boil. Reduce the heat to low and gradually add the cornmeal, whisking continuously until thickened and smooth – watch out, it might spatter and it's really hot, so wear an apron, stand back and be careful!

Once thick, add the condensed milk, cinnamon, vanilla extract, salt and a good grating of nutmeg, then stir well. If it's too thick, add a splash of water, or if you've got a bit of a sweet tooth, add a little more condensed milk. Serve straight away with a drizzle of honey and a little extra grating of nutmeg on top, and enjoy!

If for whatever reason you leave your porridge to sit before serving, it'll thicken quite a bit – to restore it to its former glory simply return to a low heat, add a splash of milk and stir until lovely and smooth again.

MUSHROOMS ON TOAST

SERVES 2

TOTAL TIME: 20 MINUTES

1 tablespoon olive oil

250g mixed mushrooms
(see tip below)

2 cloves of garlic, peeled and crushed

½ teaspoon dried chilli flakes

sea salt and freshly ground
white pepper

2 thick slices of crusty bread

1 tablespoon mascarpone

½ a bunch of fresh flat-leaf parsley,
leaves picked

juice from ½ a fat lemon
or 1 regular lemon

Place a medium frying pan over a medium heat to warm up and add the oil. Slice or tear up the mushrooms (whichever you feel like – I do both, depending on my mood). Place them in the frying pan, along with the garlic and chilli flakes. Season with salt to draw the moisture from the mushrooms – this will prevent them from being soggy and flavourless. Fry over a medium heat for 5 to 10 minutes, or until all the liquid has come out of the mushrooms and evaporated, and the mushrooms are turning lightly golden.

When the mushrooms are almost ready, toast the bread to your liking (you want hot toast to put them on!). Meanwhile, stir the mascarpone into the frying pan until all the mushrooms are well coated. Chop and add the parsley leaves with half the lemon juice, then stir together and taste. If you want more lemon or salt, this is the time to add it, along with a generous pinch of pepper (I love white pepper, but black is fine here too). Pour the mushrooms over the hot toast and serve straight away.

I like to use a mixture of chestnut and wild mushrooms (when they're in season). White mushrooms are fine, but for me, button mushrooms don't have enough flavour.

GRANOLA

100g unsalted butter, plus extra for greasing

100ml runny honey

50g light soft brown sugar

1 teaspoon vanilla extract

1 teaspoon ground cinnamon

1 teaspoon sea salt

200g mixed shelled nuts, such as pecans, almonds, hazelnuts, walnuts

800g rolled oats

150g mixed seeds, such as sunflower, pumpkin, flax, sesame, poppy

200g dried fruit, such as sour cherries, raisins, apricots, blueberries

optional: 50g dried banana chips

Preheat the oven to 200°C/400°F/gas 6. Grease a 30cm x 40cm baking tray with a little butter and line with greaseproof paper (this makes it much easier to clean up later, and everyone knows how much I hate washing up!), then set aside.

Put the butter, honey, sugar, vanilla extract, cinnamon and salt into a small pan over a low heat. Stir well and cook for a few minutes, or until melted and bubbling slightly.

Meanwhile, roughly chop the nuts, then combine with the oats and seeds in a large bowl. Pour over the melted butter mixture and stir well to coat, then tip out on to the prepared baking tray, spreading it out evenly into a nice, thin layer. Place in the hot oven for 25 to 30 minutes, or until golden and crisp, stirring every 10 minutes or so – don't worry if some bits are still a bit soft, as they will harden and crisp up once cooled. Stir in the dried fruit, then roughly chop and add the banana chips (if using). Leave to cool, then place in an airtight jar – this recipe makes 1.2kg but it'll keep for up to 4 weeks, if you can resist eating it all in the first few days!

I love this with a dollop of natural yoghurt and some **berry compote** (see page 18) or **stewed apples & pears** (see page 34), or I sometimes just grab a small handful and eat it on its own as a snack.

STEWED APPLES & PEARS

SERVES
6

TOTAL TIME: 20 MINUTES

2 large Bramley apples, peeled

2–3 large Conference pears, peeled

2 tablespoons caster sugar

1 large cinnamon stick or
1½ teaspoons ground cinnamon

50g raisins

Core the apples and pears and dice into equal-sized chunks, then place in a heavy-based pan, along with the sugar, cinnamon and 2 tablespoons of water. Stir well, then place over a low heat and simmer for 10 to 15 minutes, or until the fruit has softened, stirring in the raisins halfway through. Pick out the cinnamon stick (if using), then serve hot or cold with Greek yoghurt and **granola** (see page 32), on **sweet eggy bread** (see page 26) or swirled through my **cornmeal porridge** (see page 28).

Later in the day, serve this with ice cream or custard, or use it as a base for crumble and you've got yourself dessert!

SNACKS & QUICK FIXES

For those in-between moments when you're a little peckish – these recipes are a must in my house.

BANANA BREAD

TOTAL TIME: 1 HOUR 20 MINUTES
PLUS COOLING

190g unsalted butter, softened,
plus extra for greasing

450g self-raising flour,
plus extra for dusting

300g caster sugar

2 large free-range eggs

5 medium ripe bananas, peeled

½ teaspoon sea salt

1 whole nutmeg, for grating

2 teaspoons baking powder

190ml whole milk

1 teaspoon vanilla extract

Preheat the oven to 180°C/350°F/gas 4. Grease a 25cm x 35cm baking dish with butter and dust it with flour. Beat the butter and sugar together until pale and fluffy (I use an electric hand whisk for this, but a wooden spoon is fine – it just takes a little longer). Whisk in the eggs, then mash the bananas well and stir into the mixture, along with the salt and a few gratings of nutmeg. Sieve the flour and baking powder into a separate bowl, then fold half of it through the banana mixture. It may be a little thick, so whisk in half the milk to help loosen it up. Fold through the remaining flour, then mix in the remaining milk and the vanilla extract.

Pour the banana mixture into your prepared dish and spread it out evenly with a spatula. Bake in the hot oven for about 1 hour, or until golden and cooked through. Check if it's ready by poking a skewer into the centre – if it comes out clean, it's done, otherwise cover with tin foil and return to the oven, checking every 5 minutes or so until cooked. Leave to cool in the dish for 15 minutes, then turn out on to a wire rack to cool completely before slicing up into squares and serving with a nice glass of cold milk. Keep any leftovers in an airtight container for up to 3 days.

My children love this for an after-school treat.

JAM TARTS

MAKES
24

TOTAL TIME: 35 MINUTES

unsalted butter, for greasing

plain flour, for dusting

1 x 500g pack of shortcrust pastry

1 x 340g jar of your favourite jam,
or a mixture of whatever you
have at home

YOU NEED

2 x 12-hole fairy-cake trays

1 x 7.5cm round pastry cutter

Preheat the oven to 200°C/400°F/gas 6. Grease two 12-hole fairy-cake trays with a little butter, then set aside.

Roll out the pastry on a flour-dusted surface to about 0.5cm thick, then stamp out circles with your pastry cutter. Gently press the pastry circles into the holes of each tray, then place 1 teaspoon of jam in the middle of each one (my kids' favourites are raspberry and apricot). Place in the hot oven for about 20 minutes, or until the pastry is golden and the jam has melted slightly.

You can serve these straight away (but beware of the hot jam – I'd recommend waiting for a few minutes before tucking in) or store in an airtight container for up to 4 days.

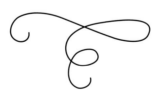

I make these jammy treats with my kids – it's a great recipe for them to help out with on a rainy afternoon – they absolutely love them and it keeps them quiet!

OAT & RAISIN COOKIES

MAKES
26

250g unsalted butter, softened,
plus extra for greasing

1 tablespoon golden syrup

200g caster sugar

2 large free-range eggs

250g plain flour,
plus extra for dusting

1 teaspoon baking powder

1 teaspoon ground cinnamon

2 teaspoons vanilla extract

350g rolled oats

300g raisins

Preheat the oven to 190°C/375°F/gas 5. Grease two large baking trays and line with greaseproof paper. In a large mixing bowl, beat the butter, golden syrup and sugar together until pale and creamy. Whisk in the eggs one at a time, then fold in all of the remaining ingredients, mixing well until you end up with a rough, sticky dough.

Dust your hands with a little flour, then take golfball-sized lumps of dough and flatten them into rounds, about 1.5cm thick. Place the rounds on the lined baking trays, leaving a 2cm space between them, and bake for about 10 minutes, or until golden and crunchy on the outside but still a little soft in the middle. Leave to cool on the trays for a few minutes, then transfer to a wire cooling rack until you're ready to tuck in. Serve with a glass of ice-cold milk, then keep any leftover cookies in an airtight container so that they keep their lovely crunch.

FRIED CHEESE SANDWICHES

SERVES
2

100g Cheddar or any
good melting cheese

4 slices of thick white bread

40g unsalted butter

Grate the cheese and divide it equally between 2 slices of bread (I prefer mature Cheddar, but it's up to you), then pop the remaining bread on top to complete your sandwiches. Melt the butter in a large non-stick frying pan over a medium-low heat. Once foaming, add the cheese sandwiches to the pan, then place a plate, bottom-side down, on top of them. Weigh the plate down by placing a couple of tins on top (this helps to seal the sandwiches and stops the cheese leaking out), then fry for 3 to 4 minutes on each side, or until golden, crisp and delicious. Serve immediately with my **roasted tomato soup** (see page 62) or just a dollop of tomato ketchup on the side, but be careful – the cheese is HOT!

Everyone I know loves a good cheese toastie. We don't have a toastie maker at home, but in my view you don't need one – this method is the perfect alternative and works every time, plus it's much easier to clean up when you're finished.

HOUMOUS
WITH CRUNCHY VEG STICKS

SERVES
8

TOTAL TIME: 10 MINUTES

2 x 400g tins of chickpeas, drained

2 tablespoons tahini

2 cloves of garlic, peeled

extra virgin olive oil

juice from ½ a lemon

sea salt and freshly ground
black pepper

1 medium cucumber

4 medium carrots, peeled

Blitz the chickpeas, tahini, garlic and 4 tablespoons of oil together in a food processor until smooth. If it's a bit thick, add 1 to 2 tablespoons more oil to get it to the consistency that looks good to you, then squeeze in the lemon juice and season to how you like it.

Halve the cucumber lengthways, then scoop out and discard the watery bits in the middle. Slice the cucumber and carrots into batons, then serve with the houmous and get dipping!

Warmed wholemeal pitta breads, sliced into strips, are great for dipping in houmous too. My kids like all kinds of stuff with it – let them get creative and choose different vegetables to dip and dunk, as long as it's got a good crunch, any vegetable will work, and it's a great way to get them to eat more veg and to try new things.

JAMAICAN PATTIES
2 WAYS

SERVES
4

FOR THE PASTRY

300g plain flour

½ tablespoon ground turmeric

sea salt and freshly ground
black pepper

125g cold unsalted butter, cubed

CHOOSE YOUR FILLING:

FOR THE BEEF FILLING

4 spring onions, trimmed

½ a Scotch bonnet chilli, deseeded

4 sprigs of fresh thyme, leaves picked

1½ tablespoons curry powder

300g beef mince

30g fresh breadcrumbs

FOR THE SALTFISH FILLING

250g boneless, skinless
saltfish fillets

1 medium onion, peeled

2 mixed-colour peppers, deseeded

2 cloves of garlic, peeled

½ a Scotch bonnet chilli, deseeded

4 sprigs of fresh thyme, leaves picked

2 medium ripe tomatoes

FOR THE PASTRY: Sieve the flour, turmeric, a pinch of pepper and 1 teaspoon of salt into a large bowl. Use your fingertips to gently rub in the butter until it looks like breadcrumbs. Gradually mix in 110ml of ice-cold water until it forms a soft dough then wrap in clingfilm and rest in the fridge for at least 30 minutes.

FOR THE BEEF FILLING: Finely slice the spring onions and chilli and put into a non-stick frying pan over a medium-low heat with 1 tablespoon of oil and the thyme. Fry for 2 minutes, or until soft, then stir in the curry powder for another minute. Turn the heat up to medium-high and fry the mince for about 5 minutes, or until browned all over. Add the breadcrumbs and 200ml of boiling water, then cook over a medium-low heat for 10 minutes, or until thickened. Season to how you like it and leave to cool.

FOR THE SALTFISH FILLING: Rinse the saltfish under cold, running water, then put into a pan of cold water and bring to the boil over a high heat. Drain, return to the pan with fresh cold water and bring to the boil again. Simmer for 10 minutes, or until softened, then drain. Meanwhile, finely chop the onion, peppers, garlic and chilli, then fry in a non-stick frying pan over a medium-low heat with 1 tablespoon of oil and the thyme for 10 minutes, or until soft. Dice and add the tomatoes, then fry for 5 minutes on a medium heat, or until jammy. Flake and stir in the fish, then leave to cool.

To make the patties, preheat the oven to 200°C/400°F/gas 6. Divide the pastry into four and roll into 1cm-thick equal-sized rounds, using an 18cm saucer as a template to cut them out. Divide your chosen filling between them, placing onto one half of each pastry circle, then carefully fold the other side up and over the filling and seal the edges together with a fork. Pierce the patties, place on a lined baking tray and bake for 20 to 25 minutes, or until crisp and golden. Freeze any cooked leftover patties, then simply defrost and reheat in the oven for 20 minutes at 180°C/350°F/gas 4 another day.

MENEMEN (TURKISH-STYLE EGGS)

SERVES
6

TOTAL TIME: 30 MINUTES

4 fresh Turkish long green chillies
or 1 regular green chilli

1 red pepper, deseeded

1 yellow pepper, deseeded

1 medium onion, peeled

olive oil

5 large ripe tomatoes

sea salt and freshly ground
black pepper

6 large free-range eggs

½ a bunch of fresh flat-leaf parsley,
leaves picked

TO SERVE

1 loaf of crusty bread

Chop each chilli into three equal-sized chunks (I leave the seeds in, but deseed if you prefer). Roughly chop the peppers and onion into 2cm chunks. Place the chopped vegetables and chillies in a large non-stick ovenproof frying pan over a medium-high heat with 1 tablespoon of oil and fry for around 5 minutes, or until softened (you don't want them to colour just yet).

Coarsely grate 3 tomatoes into the pan, discarding the skins, then stir well and reduce the heat to low. Cut the remaining tomatoes into wedges and add to the pan with a splash of water. Season to how you like it and let it bubble away for 5 to 10 minutes, or until the tomato wedges are softened but still holding their shape.

Preheat the grill to a medium-high heat. Make six small wells in the tomato mixture with a spoon. Crack an egg into each well and cook for a further 2 minutes over a low heat, or until the eggs start to set underneath. Transfer the pan to the grill for 1 to 2 minutes, or until the whites are cooked, but the yolks are still runny. Roughly chop and scatter over the parsley leaves, then serve the pan in the middle of the table with some good old crusty bread and let everyone get stuck in. They will love it!

My best friend, Cicek, is Turkish and she always cooks this for me – if you like runny eggs and chilli, this will change your life!

PIZZA - YOUR WAY

MAKES 4

TOTAL TIME: 40 MINUTES,
PLUS PROVING

FOR THE PIZZA DOUGH

500g strong bread flour,
plus extra for dusting

1½ x 7g sachets of dried yeast

½ tablespoon caster sugar

1 heaped teaspoon fine sea salt

olive oil

FOR THE QUICK TOMATO SAUCE

2 cloves of garlic, peeled

1 bunch of fresh basil

1 tablespoon tomato purée

1 teaspoon dried oregano

1 x 400g tin of chopped tomatoes

1 teaspoon caster sugar

sea salt and freshly ground
black pepper

FOR THE TOPPING

2 x 125g balls of mozzarella cheese

your favourite toppings, such as
Parma ham, leftover roast chicken,
sweetcorn, olives, sliced onions,
chillies, mushrooms, peppers

Put the flour into a large bowl and make a well in the middle. Mix the yeast with 300ml of lukewarm water, then add to the well with the sugar, salt and 1½ tablespoons of oil. Mix together with a fork, gradually incorporating the flour until you have a sticky dough – if it's a little dry, add a splash more water. Bring it together with your hands, then knead well for 5 to 10 minutes, or until smooth and stretchy. Place in a lightly oiled bowl, cover with a damp tea towel and put in a warm place for 30 minutes, or until doubled in size.

Now for the quick tomato sauce (or you could use my **hidden vegetable pasta sauce** from page 78 if you have some). Finely chop the garlic and basil (including the stalks). Put the garlic into a frying pan over a medium heat with 1 tablespoon of oil. Stir in the tomato purée and oregano and fry for about 30 seconds, then add the chopped basil, tomatoes and sugar. Bring to the boil, then reduce to a low heat and simmer for 10 minutes, or until thickened and reduced. Season to how you like it, then remove from the heat and set aside.

Preheat the oven to 220°C/425°F/gas 7. Knock back the dough and knead for a few minutes, then divide into four equal-sized balls. On a flour-dusted surface, roll into circles about 0.5cm thick, then divide between two large flour-dusted baking trays (if you're only making a couple of pizzas, wrap the remaining rounds in clingfilm and freeze them for another time – they'll take just 5 minutes longer to cook from frozen). Spread about 4 tablespoons of the tomato sauce onto each round, then tear over the mozzarella and scatter over your favourite toppings – choose whatever you like, just keep it simple and be careful not to overload them! Place in the hot oven for 10 to 12 minutes, or until golden and bubbling, then serve straight away.

MACKEREL
IN SPICY TOMATO SAUCE

SERVES
4-6

TOTAL TIME: 20 MINUTES

1 medium onion, peeled

1 red pepper, deseeded

2 large ripe tomatoes

1 fresh red chilli, deseeded

1 tablespoon olive oil

2 cloves of garlic, peeled and crushed

2 sprigs of fresh thyme, leaves picked

3 x 125g tins of mackerel fillets in tomato sauce

sea salt and freshly ground black pepper

Finely slice the onion and pepper. Dice the tomatoes and finely chop the chilli. Place a frying pan on a medium heat to warm up then add the oil. Add the chopped vegetables, chilli, garlic and thyme leaves and fry for 5 to 10 minutes, or until soft and jammy, stirring occasionally. Stir in the mackerel (including the tomato sauce) and allow to warm through. Season to how you like it, then serve with rice, pasta or crusty bread, and a nice green side salad.

My kids love mackerel, but you can swap in other tinned fish if you prefer – tuna, salmon or sardines will all work great. This is the best quick fix when you've had a busy day, have nothing you've pre-prepared in the freezer, and you need something tasty, fast.

SPICY PRAWNS

SERVES
2

TOTAL TIME: 25 MINUTES

4 spring onions, trimmed

2 fresh red chillies

2 cloves of garlic, peeled

½ a bunch of fresh flat-leaf parsley

1 tablespoon olive oil

2 medium ripe tomatoes

12 frozen raw king prawns, unpeeled

zest and juice from
1 unwaxed lemon

sea salt and freshly ground
black pepper

TO SERVE

crusty bread

Finely slice the spring onions and chillies at an angle, then finely chop the garlic and parsley stalks (reserving the leaves for later). Put it all into a deep frying pan or a wok over a medium heat with the oil, then fry for about 3 minutes, or until softened and starting to brown. Coarsely grate in the tomatoes, discarding the skins, and cook for a further 2 minutes, stirring continuously. Add the frozen prawns and fry for 7 to 10 minutes, or until pink, cooked through and piping hot.

Roughly chop the parsley leaves and add to the pan along with the zest and juice from the lemon, then season and toss together well. Serve immediately, with a chunk of crusty bread to mop up all the yummy juices, and with a crisp green salad on the side.

My husband came home one day with these spicy prawns and they tasted like the best things I'd ever eaten – this is my version of that recipe for all of you to enjoy at home.

BATCH COOKING

I don't buy ready meals – I make them! I tend to put aside a few hours on a Saturday (Sunday is football time), cook up a couple of these recipes, then box or bag them up in portions, label and freeze them. With baked recipes, I divide and layer up a batch between foil containers (which you'll find in good pound shops or supermarkets), before freezing them. Just make sure you defrost thoroughly before cooking (I take them out the night before I need them and pop them in the fridge overnight). Cook until piping hot the whole way through, remembering to adjust the cooking times depending on the size of your portions. When working full time and on a tight budget, batch cooking is the best way to make sure you're eating good stuff all the time.

CHILLI CON VEGGIE

SERVES 10

2 medium onions, peeled

4 cloves of garlic, peeled

1 medium leek, trimmed

1 long fresh red chilli

2 tablespoons olive oil

2 tablespoons ground cumin

2 tablespoons ground coriander

2 tablespoons smoked paprika

½ a cinnamon stick or
1 teaspoon ground cinnamon

2 tablespoons dried oregano

1 whole nutmeg, for grating

2 tablespoons tomato purée

250g dried green lentils

250g dried red lentils

2 x 400g tins of red kidney beans,
drained and rinsed

2 x 400g tins of black beans,
drained and rinsed

2 x 400g tins of chopped tomatoes

1.2 litres organic vegetable stock

sea salt and freshly ground
black pepper

Finely chop the onions, garlic, leek and chilli (I leave the seeds in, but deseed if you prefer) and place into your largest, heavy-based pan over a medium heat with the oil. Fry for about 5 minutes, or until softened. Add the spices, dried herbs and a good grating of nutmeg, then fry for 2 minutes – if it's a little dry at this point, simply add a splash of water to help it out. Stir in the tomato purée and cook for a further 2 minutes.

Stir in the lentils, beans and chopped tomatoes, then add the stock (I try to use homemade stock, but if you've only got stock cubes, that's fine too). Bring it all to the boil, then reduce to a low heat and let it bubble away for at least 1 hour, or until thickened and reduced, stirring every 15 to 20 minutes, then season to how you like it. I like this with rice or on a jacket potato, scattered with coriander leaves and with lime wedges and a dollop of soured cream on the side. This is one of my all-time favourite dinners.

ROASTED TOMATO SOUP

SERVES 8

TOTAL TIME: 1 HOUR 30 MINUTES

2kg ripe tomatoes, on the vine

1 whole bulb of garlic

8–10 sprigs of fresh thyme

sea salt and freshly ground
black pepper

4 tablespoons olive oil

1.7 litres organic chicken or
vegetable stock

1 bunch of fresh basil, leaves picked

Preheat the oven to 220°C/425°F/gas 7. Halve the tomatoes and evenly spread them out, cut side up, in a sturdy baking tray. Add the vines for extra flavour as they roast, then halve the bulb of garlic across the middle and add that with the thyme sprigs, season well and drizzle over the oil. Roast for 25 to 30 minutes, or until soft, sticky and starting to turn golden around the edges.

Transfer the roasted tomatoes into a large heavy-based pan, removing and throwing away the thyme sprigs and vines. Squeeze the soft garlic from its skin and add the flesh to the pan, then place over a high heat and pour in the stock (I try to use homemade stock, but if you've only got stock cubes, that's fine too). Bring to the boil, then reduce the heat to medium-low and let it bubble away for about 20 minutes, or until reduced slightly. Stir in most of the basil leaves, then blitz with a hand blender until smooth. Simmer gently over a low heat for a further 25 to 30 minutes, or until thickened, stirring occasionally – if it's too thick simply loosen with a splash of hot water from the kettle. Divide between bowls, then scatter over the reserved basil leaves and serve. This is delicious with my **fried cheese sandwiches** (see page 44) on the side for dunking.

Basil oil goes down really well with this soup – to make your own simply blitz the leaves from a large bunch of fresh basil with 6 tablespoons of extra virgin olive oil in a blender. Season to how you like it, then drizzle over your soup before serving. Keep any leftover oil in a jar and drizzle over risottos or pasta dishes, or use as a dressing for my **tasty side salad** (see page 106).

BEEF STEW & DUMPLINGS

SERVES 10

TOTAL TIME: 2 HOURS 50 MINUTES

1kg stewing beef

1 tablespoon plain flour

sea salt and freshly ground
black pepper

olive oil

2 medium onions, peeled

2 leeks, trimmed

4 sprigs of fresh thyme

3 organic beef stock cubes

3 large carrots, peeled

1.2kg potatoes, scrubbed clean

125g pearl barley

FOR THE DUMPLINGS

250g self-raising flour

125g beef or vegetable suet or
cold unsalted butter

This recipe makes enough for 10 – if you're freezing a batch, it's best to leave the dumplings raw. They'll cook happily from frozen in your leftover stew next time.

Chop the beef into rough 5cm chunks, put into a large bowl with the flour and a big pinch of salt and pepper, and toss well to coat. In batches, fry the beef in your largest pan over a medium heat with a splash of oil for about 5 minutes, or until browned all over, stirring occasionally. Repeat until all the beef is browned, transferring it to a plate as you go. Meanwhile, roughly chop the onions and leeks.

Return the pan to the heat and add the onions, leeks, thyme sprigs and another splash of oil. Fry for about 5 minutes, or until softened, then stir in the browned beef. Cover with water (you'll need about 1.4 litres), crumble in the stock cubes and bring to the boil. Reduce the heat to low, cover and let it bubble away for about 1 hour 30 minutes, or until the beef is tender.

When the time's up, chop the carrots and potatoes into 2cm chunks and add to the pan with the pearl barley. Stir well and simmer for about 30 minutes, or until the vegetables are cooked.

Meanwhile, make the dumplings. Put the flour and a pinch of salt into a large bowl, then stir in the suet or rub in the butter. Add 1½ tablespoons of cold water, stirring continuously with a knife until you have a rough dough – try to handle it as little as possible so you get light, fluffy dumplings. Take lumps of dough and roll into 10 golfball-sized balls (you don't want them any bigger – they're going to swell to almost double the size!). Carefully drop the dumplings into the stew (you may need to add a splash more water because the dough will suck up a lot of liquid) and simmer for a further 20 to 25 minutes, or until the dumplings are big, fluffy and have floated to the surface. Fish out and throw away the thyme sprigs, then serve and enjoy!

COTTAGE PIE

SERVES 8

TOTAL TIME: 1 HOUR 35 MINUTES

800g beef mince

2 medium onions, peeled

2 cloves of garlic, peeled

1 leek, trimmed

½ a bunch of fresh thyme,
leaves picked

1–2 fresh bay leaves

250g closed cup or
chestnut mushrooms

2 large carrots, peeled

2 tablespoons plain flour

2 organic beef stock cubes

300g frozen peas

sea salt and freshly ground
black pepper

2 x **cheesy mash** (see page 116)

50g Cheddar cheese

Preheat the oven to 200°C/400°F/gas 6. Place a very large, shallow pan over a medium heat. In batches, fry the mince for about 5 minutes, or until browned all over and most of the liquid has evaporated. Meanwhile, finely chop the onions, garlic and leek. When it's all nicely browned, return all the mince to the pan, add the chopped vegetables, thyme and bay leaves and fry for another 5 minutes, or until softened, stirring occasionally. Finely slice and add the mushrooms, then fry for a further 6 minutes, or until all the water has come out of the mushrooms and evaporated.

Finely slice and stir in the carrots, then add the flour and crumble in the stock cubes. Add just enough water to cover (you'll need about 600ml) and bring to the boil, then reduce the heat to low and let it bubble away for 25 minutes, or until the beef is tender and the sauce has thickened and reduced to a nice gravy consistency.

Stir in the peas (I like petits pois, but use any you like) and season to how you like it, then transfer to a 25cm x 30cm baking dish – fish out and throw away the bay leaf. Top with the **cheesy mash** and grate over the cheese (I prefer mature Cheddar, but it's up to you). Cook in the oven for 25 to 30 minutes, or until golden and bubbling. Leave to stand for 10 minutes, then serve with seasonal greens.

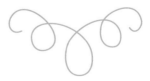

POTATO, CHICKPEA & CAULIFLOWER CURRY

SERVES 6-8

TOTAL TIME: 50 MINUTES

1 large onion, peeled

2 cloves of garlic, peeled

5cm piece of ginger, peeled

1 long fresh red chilli

2 tablespoons olive oil

2 tablespoons curry powder

1 teaspoon ground cumin

1 teaspoon ground coriander

1 teaspoon black mustard seeds

1 medium cauliflower (500g)

400g potatoes, scrubbed clean

1 tablespoon tomato purée

1 x 400g tin of chopped tomatoes

1 litre organic chicken
or vegetable stock

2 x 400g tins of chickpeas, drained

juice from 1 fat lemon

sea salt and freshly ground
black pepper

½ a bunch of fresh coriander,
leaves picked

TO SERVE

Greek yoghurt

Finely slice the onion, garlic, ginger and chilli (I leave the seeds in, but deseed if you prefer) and place in a very large, heavy-based pan over a medium heat with the oil and all of the spices. Fry gently for about 5 minutes, or until softened, stirring regularly. Meanwhile, break the cauliflower into florets, discarding the stalk, then chop the potatoes into 2.5cm chunks.

Stir the tomato purée into the pan and fry for a further 2 minutes, then add the chopped tomatoes and stock (I try to use homemade stock, but if you've only got stock cubes, that's fine too), along with the cauliflower, potatoes and chickpeas. Bring it all to the boil, then cover and reduce to a simmer for about 35 minutes, or until the potatoes and cauliflower are cooked through. Squeeze in the lemon juice and season to how you like it (it's important to season this right at the end – the sauce will thicken and intensify in flavour as it cooks, so you might find it's salty enough already). Scatter over the coriander leaves and serve with a bowl of yoghurt. I like this with basmati rice and warm naan bread too.

I've used fresh cauliflower here, but you can always use 500g of frozen cauliflower instead – it'll work just as well. Sometimes I also like to swap out some of the cauliflower for broccoli, okra or butternut squash, or stir a bit of spinach through it at the end – make use of whatever you've got in the fridge.

MAJESTICAL MAC 'N' CHEESE

SERVES
10

TOTAL TIME: 50 MINUTES

1kg dried macaroni pasta

sea salt and freshly ground
black pepper

100g unsalted butter

100g plain flour

1.2 litres semi-skimmed milk

500g Cheddar cheese

2 tablespoons English mustard

1 whole nutmeg, for grating

optional: 1 handful of
stale breadcrumbs

Preheat the oven to 220°C/425°F/gas 7. Cook the macaroni in a pan of boiling salted water for 8 to 10 minutes, or until al dente (it'll continue cooking in the oven, so don't overdo it now).

Meanwhile, melt the butter in a pan over a medium heat, then whisk in the flour until well combined (you'll end up with what looks like a lump of dough – this is called the roux). Gradually add the milk a splash at a time, whisking continuously until any lumps have disappeared and you have a smooth white sauce – you may not need to add all the milk, so use your brain and stop when it's looking good. Grate in two-thirds of the cheese (I prefer mature Cheddar, but it's up to you) and stir well until melted, then mix in the mustard and a few gratings of nutmeg and season to how you like it.

Drain the pasta and stir into the sauce to coat, then tip into a 30cm x 35cm baking dish. Grate over the remaining cheese, sprinkle over the breadcrumbs (if using) and bake in the oven for 25 to 30 minutes, or until golden and bubbling. Serve with a green salad, and I sometimes have baked beans on the side too.

This is quite simply the most majestical of all comfort foods – it works its magic every time when you're in need of a feel-good, hearty dinner. I sometimes like to swap 500g of pasta for the same amount of blanched cauliflower, to make it into mac 'n' cauliflower cheese!

EASY CHICKEN CURRY

SERVES 8

TOTAL TIME: 1 HOUR 45 MINUTES
PLUS MARINATING

2 large onions, peeled

6 cloves of garlic, peeled

3 mixed-colour peppers, deseeded

2 large carrots, peeled

750g potatoes, peeled

6 higher-welfare skinless, boneless chicken breasts or 8 higher-welfare skinless, boneless chicken thighs

3 tablespoons curry powder

1½ teaspoons ground cumin

1 teaspoon ground coriander

1 teaspoon garam masala

2 sprigs of fresh thyme

olive oil

sea salt and freshly ground black pepper

1 litre organic chicken stock

1 bunch of fresh coriander, leaves picked

Finely slice the onions, garlic and peppers. Dice the carrots and chop the potatoes into 2.5cm chunks, then place it all in a large bowl. Chop the chicken into rough 2.5cm pieces and add to the vegetables with the spices, thyme sprigs, 1 tablespoon of oil and a pinch of salt and pepper. Using your hands, mix well to coat, then cover and place in the fridge to marinate for at least 30 minutes, though I prefer to leave it overnight.

When you're ready to cook, heat 2 tablespoons of oil in your largest heavy-based pan over a high heat, then pick out and add half the chicken. Fry for about 5 minutes, or until golden all over, turning occasionally. Remove to a plate and repeat with the remaining chicken, adding a splash more oil to the pan, if needed, then set aside. Return the pan to a medium heat, add 1 tablespoon of oil and all the chopped vegetables and thyme, then cook for 8 to 10 minutes, or until the onions are softened.

Stir the chicken back into the pan and pour in the stock (I try to use homemade stock, but if you've only got stock cubes, that's fine too). Turn the heat up to high and bring to the boil, then reduce to a gentle simmer for 40 to 50 minutes, or until thickened and reduced. Fish out and throw away the thyme sprigs, season to how you like it, then divide between plates and scatter over the coriander leaves. Delicious served with basmati rice and a dollop of natural yoghurt.

LASAGNE

SERVES
8

500g lamb or higher-welfare
pork mince

500g beef mince

1.5 litres **hidden vegetable pasta
sauce** (see page 78)

85g unsalted butter

85g plain flour

850ml whole milk

1 whole nutmeg, for grating

sea salt and freshly ground
black pepper

250g dried lasagne sheets

100g Cheddar cheese

Preheat the oven to 200°C/400°F/gas 6. Place a very large non-stick pan over a medium heat. In batches, fry the mince for 5 to 10 minutes, or until browned all over and most of the liquid has evaporated, stirring occasionally. Return all the meat to the pan along with the **hidden vegetable pasta sauce** and simmer for 15 to 20 minutes – this is your Bolognese sauce.

Meanwhile, melt the butter in a pan over a medium heat, then whisk in the flour until well combined (you'll end up with what looks like a lump of dough – this is called the roux). Gradually add the milk a splash at a time, whisking continuously until any lumps have disappeared and you have a smooth white sauce – you may not need to add all the milk, so use your brain and stop when it's looking good. Mix in a good grating of nutmeg and season to how you like it.

Now, to build the lasagne, season the Bolognese sauce to how you like it, then use one-third of it to cover the base of a 25cm x 30cm baking dish. Spoon over roughly one-quarter of the white sauce (this is called béchamel), then top with an even layer of lasagne sheets. Repeat twice more, then spoon over the remaining béchamel, grate over the cheese (I prefer mature Cheddar, but it's up to you), and bake in the oven for 35 to 40 minutes, or until golden and bubbling on top and the pasta is cooked through (you can check by sticking a knife into the lasagne – if it goes in easily, it's ready). Serve with a side salad and if you're feeling naughty, my **garlic bread** (see pages 124–125) too.

FISH PIE

SERVES
8

1 bunch of fresh flat-leaf parsley

1.2 litres whole milk

¼ of a medium onion, peeled

1 fresh bay leaf

4 black peppercorns

320g frozen white fish fillets

320g frozen salmon fillets

80g unsalted butter

80g plain flour

zest and juice from 1 unwaxed lemon

300g frozen peeled cooked prawns

300g frozen peas

sea salt and freshly ground
black pepper

2 x **basic mash** (see page 116)

Preheat the oven to 220°C/425°F/gas 7. Pick the parsley leaves and set aside for later, then tie the stalks together with string and place in a large pan over a medium heat with the milk, onion, bay leaf, peppercorns and fish fillets. Simmer gently for about 15 minutes, or until the fish is cooked through. Using a slotted spoon, remove the fish to a plate and leave to cool. Carefully strain the milk through a sieve into another pan and put to one side.

Melt the butter in a pan over a medium heat, then whisk in the flour, until well combined (you'll end up with what looks like a lump of dough – this is called the roux). Gradually add the warm milk a splash at a time, whisking continuously until any lumps have disappeared and you have a smooth white sauce – you may not need to add all the milk, so use your brain and stop when it's looking good. Add the lemon zest and juice, then roughly chop and add the parsley leaves, stir in the prawns and peas (I like petits pois, but any peas will do) and add a pinch of salt and pepper.

Flake the fish into a 25cm x 30cm baking dish, spoon over the sauce and top with my **basic mash**. Roughly smooth it out to the edges, then use a spoon to scuff it up – this will make it look lovely, textured, and much more appealing for the kids! Bake in the oven for about 25 minutes, or until golden and bubbling at the edges. Serve with steamed broccoli or a crisp green salad.

HIDDEN VEGETABLE PASTA SAUCE

3 LITRES

TOTAL TIME: 2 HOURS

2 medium onions, peeled

4 cloves of garlic, peeled

1 large leek, trimmed

3 medium carrots, peeled

2 sticks of celery, trimmed

2 tablespoons olive oil

250g closed cup or chestnut mushrooms

2 medium courgettes

2 medium aubergines

1 tablespoon dried oregano

4 tablespoons tomato purée

1 fresh bay leaf

2 x 400g tins of chopped tomatoes or 2 x 500g cartons of passata

1 teaspoon caster sugar

850ml organic vegetable stock

sea salt and freshly ground black pepper

Very roughly chop the onions, garlic, leek, carrots and celery, then blitz in a food processor until finely chopped (if you want your sauce a little chunkier, coarsely grate them instead, using a box grater). Heat the oil in your largest heavy-based pan over a medium heat, then add the onion mixture and fry for 10 minutes, or until softened, stirring occasionally.

Meanwhile, finely chop the remaining vegetables (again, coarsely grate or roughly chop by hand for a chunkier sauce), then add to the pan and fry over a low heat for a further 20 minutes, or until softened, stirring occasionally. Stir in the oregano, tomato purée and bay leaf, fry for 2 to 3 minutes, then pour in the chopped tomatoes or passata. Add the sugar and vegetable stock (I try to use homemade stock, but if you've only got stock cubes, that's fine too), then cover and let it bubble away over a low heat for 30 minutes to 1 hour, stirring occasionally – the longer you cook it, the more the flavour will develop as it reduces and thickens.

When it's ready, fish out the bay leaf and season to how you like it (it's important to season this right at the end – the sauce will thicken and intensify in flavour as it cooks, so you might find it's salty enough already). Divide the sauce between freezer-proof containers and leave to cool, then label and pop into the freezer for up to 3 months, to use whenever you like. This is great as a simple pasta sauce or in my **lasagne** (see page 74), with **simple spaghetti & meatballs** (see page 84) or as a tasty base for **pizza** (see page 52).

This is my all-time favourite recipe and a great way to get my kids eating vegetables. If you have a couple of fresh rosemary or thyme sprigs lying around, chuck them in too for added flavour.

DINNER TIME

Dinner time is the one point when we're all in the same place at the same time – I'll cook something nice and we'll sit down together and find out all about each other's day.

SIMPLE SPAGHETTI & MEATBALLS

SERVES 4

TOTAL TIME: 55 MINUTES

12 cream crackers

1 teaspoon dried oregano

1 teaspoon smoked paprika

1 teaspoon ground cumin

sea salt and freshly ground
black pepper

250g beef mince

250g lamb or higher-welfare
pork mince

1 large free-range egg

1 litre **hidden vegetable pasta
sauce** (see page 78)

olive oil

320g dried spaghetti

extra virgin olive oil

TO SERVE

optional: Parmesan cheese

Bunch up the crackers in a clean tea towel, then bash to small crumbs with a rolling pin. Combine with the oregano, paprika, cumin and a pinch of salt and pepper in a large bowl. Add all the mince and crack in the egg, then scrunch and mix together with your hands (it's quite therapeutic!). Divide the mixture into 16 pieces and roll into golfball-sized meatballs.

Simmer the **hidden vegetable pasta sauce** in a large pan over a low heat – if it's a little thick, add a splash of water from the kettle to loosen. Meanwhile, heat a drizzle of olive oil in a large non-stick frying pan over a medium heat. Once hot, add the meatballs (you may need to do this in batches) and fry for 5 to 10 minutes, or until browned all over, giving the pan a good shake from time to time. Tip the meatballs into the sauce, then cover and let it bubble away for a further 25 minutes, or until the meatballs are cooked through.

When there's about 10 minutes remaining, cook the spaghetti in boiling salted water, according to the packet instructions. Drain the pasta, toss it in a drizzle of extra virgin olive oil, then divide between bowls. Ladle over the meatballs and sauce and serve with a grating of Parmesan, if you like.

> For the best, most beautiful-tasting meatballs,
> I use a mixture of beef and lamb or pork mince,
> but you can just use one type, if you prefer.

HOMEMADE FISH FINGERS
& MINTY SMASHED PEAS

SERVES
4

TOTAL TIME: 30 MINUTES

450g frozen white fish fillets

500g frozen peas

5 tablespoons plain flour

1 tablespoon smoked paprika

zest and juice from ½ an
unwaxed lemon

sea salt and freshly ground
black pepper

2 large free-range eggs

3 slices of wholemeal bread (100g)

sunflower oil

½ a bunch of fresh mint,
leaves picked

Start by defrosting the fish fillets, preferably overnight in the fridge (I like cod or haddock, but it's up to you what you use).

Put the peas into a colander in the sink and pour over boiling water to defrost them, then set aside. Place the flour in a shallow bowl with the paprika, lemon zest and a pinch of salt and pepper, then beat the eggs in another shallow bowl. Blitz the bread in a food processor to fine breadcrumbs, then tip onto a plate. Once defrosted, slice the fillets lengthways into fingers, roughly 2cm wide, then add to the flour and toss to coat (you'll need to do this in batches). Dip the flour-dusted fish pieces into the egg, shake off the excess, then roll in the breadcrumbs until well coated and place on a tray.

Heat 1 tablespoon of oil in a large non-stick frying pan over a medium heat. Add the fish fingers (you'll need to do this in batches) and fry for 2 to 3 minutes on each side, or until golden, crispy and cooked through. Remove to a double layer of kitchen paper to drain while you fry the next batch, adding a splash more oil, if needed.

Meanwhile, blitz the peas in a food processor until they're smashed up to a nice, chunky purée, or mash well with a fork. Tip into a bowl, then finely chop and add the mint leaves, squeeze in the lemon juice and season to how you like it. Mix well and serve alongside the crispy fish fingers and a nice green salad. If you want a dollop of ketchup too, I won't judge!

ROAST CHICKEN DINNER

SERVES
4-6

TOTAL TIME: 2 HOURS

1 medium onion, peeled
(keep the trimmings)

1 large carrot, peeled
(keep the trimmings)

1 stick of celery, trimmed
(keep the trimmings)

1 bulb of garlic

2 fresh bay leaves

4 sprigs of fresh thyme

½ a bunch of fresh flat-leaf parsley

1 x 1.5kg higher-welfare
whole chicken

20g unsalted butter

sea salt and freshly ground
black pepper

1 organic chicken stock cube

1 heaped tablespoon plain flour

This is a regular favourite in my house – and the most important rule for a good roast is to always, always make your own gravy!

Preheat the oven to 200°C/400°F/gas 6. Roughly chop the onion, carrot and celery, then spread out across a heavy roasting tray. Halve the garlic bulb across the middle and add to the tray with the herbs. Trim off the chicken wing tips, parson's nose and any loose bits of skin, then set these aside. Rub the butter all over the chicken and season with plenty of salt and pepper, then place in the tray on top of the veg and roast for about 1 hour 20 minutes, or until cooked through. Now's a good time to get on with any sides – I like **roast potatoes** (see page 120), **honey & cumin-roasted carrots** (see page 122) and some steamed greens (prep the greens now but they won't need cooking until later).

Meanwhile, make the gravy stock. Put 1.2 litres of cold water into a medium pan and place over a high heat. Add the chicken offcuts and vegetable trimmings (if you're cooking other veg to go with your roast, use these trimmings too – the only peelings I don't use are potato ones). Bring to the boil, then crumble in the stock cube and reduce to a gentle simmer until needed.

To check if the chicken is ready, pierce the thickest part of a thigh with a knife – if the juices run clear, it's done. Remove to a board, cover with tin foil and a clean tea towel and leave to rest for 20 to 30 minutes. Meanwhile, pick out and discard the garlic, then place the tray over a medium-high heat on the hob. Mash everything up with a potato masher, scraping all the nice bits from the bottom of the tray as you go. Stir in the flour, then pour in the stock and bring to the boil. Keep stirring and mashing everything together until it's thickened and looking like the best gravy you've ever made, then strain into a pan, season to how you like it and place over a low heat to simmer until needed. Carve up the chicken and serve with your homemade gravy and all the trimmings.

MY MUM'S
CHICKEN & VEGETABLE SOUP

SERVES 8

1 x 1.5kg higher-welfare
whole chicken

3 medium carrots, peeled
(keep the trimmings)

1 large leek, trimmed

4 cloves of garlic, peeled

1 large onion, peeled

1 tablespoon olive oil

1 large sprig of fresh thyme

½ a butternut squash
(350g), deseeded

500g potatoes, scrubbed clean

2 organic chicken stock cubes

sea salt and freshly ground
black pepper

1 x 200g bag of baby spinach

optional: 1–2 fresh red chillies

Trim off the chicken wing tips, parson's nose and any loose bits of skin, then place these in a large, deep casserole pan with the whole chicken. Add the carrot trimmings, then place over a high heat and pour in just enough water to cover the chicken. Put the lid on and bring to the boil, then reduce the heat to low and let it bubble away for about 1 hour, or until cooked through. To check if the chicken is ready, pierce the thickest part of a thigh with a knife – if the juices run clear, it's done. Carefully transfer to a board to cool, then sieve the stock into a large bowl, discarding the trimmings.

Finely slice the leek and garlic, then roughly chop the onion and carrots. Return the casserole pan to a medium heat, add the oil along with the chopped vegetables and thyme sprig, then fry for about 5 minutes, or until softened. Meanwhile, chop the squash and potatoes into 1.5cm chunks, then stir into the pan. Pour in the homemade chicken stock, crumble in the stock cubes and bring to the boil. Reduce the heat to low and simmer gently for 15 to 20 minutes, or until the potatoes are tender.

Meanwhile, carve up the chicken, pulling all the meat away from the carcass and shredding it into the soup, discarding the skin and wobbly bits (if the chicken's too hot to handle, wear rubber gloves!). Simmer for a further 5 minutes to warm the chicken through, then season to how you like it. Just before serving, pick out the thyme sprig, then stir through the spinach (adding it at the end will stop it disintegrating into the soup) and serve with lots of chopped chilli on top, if you like.

My kids call this recipe 'Nanny's soup for poorly people' because my mum always makes it for us when we're ill – when I was a kid, it used to make me feel better in no time at all, and it still does!

CHICKEN & MUSHROOM PIE

SERVES 4

TOTAL TIME: 1 HOUR 25 MINUTES

4 higher-welfare skinless, boneless chicken breasts or 6 higher-welfare skinless, boneless chicken thighs

sea salt and freshly ground black pepper

olive oil

2 medium leeks, trimmed

500g closed cup or chestnut mushrooms

2 cloves of garlic, peeled

2 sprigs of fresh thyme, leaves picked

1 tablespoon plain flour

600ml organic chicken stock

250g mascarpone

½ a bunch of fresh flat-leaf parsley, leaves picked

1 large free-range egg yolk, beaten

plain flour, for dusting

1 x 500g pack of puff pastry

Preheat the oven to 200°C/400°F/gas 6. Chop the chicken into rough 2.5cm pieces and season with salt and pepper. Heat 2 tablespoons of oil in a large shallow pan over a medium heat, then add the chicken (you may need to do this in batches). Fry for about 5 minutes, or until golden all over, turning occasionally. Meanwhile, finely slice the leeks, mushrooms and garlic. Remove the chicken to a double layer of kitchen paper to drain, then set aside.

Return the pan to a high heat and add the chopped vegetables, garlic and thyme leaves. Fry for about 10 minutes, or until the liquid has come out of the mushrooms and evaporated, and the vegetables have softened. Stir in the chicken pieces and the flour, then pour in the stock (I try to use homemade stock, but if you've only got stock cubes, that's fine too). Bring to the boil, then lower to a simmer for around 20 minutes, or until reduced by a quarter. Stir in the mascarpone until it melts and you have a nice creamy sauce, then roughly chop and add the parsley leaves. Season to how you like it, then place in a 20cm baking dish and leave to cool for 10 minutes or so.

Brush the rim of the dish with a little beaten egg yolk. On a flour-dusted surface, roll out the pastry to about 1cm thick, then loosely roll it up around the rolling pin, hold it over the dish and carefully unroll it over the top. Trim off any excess bits and pinch the edges to seal (I like to use the scraps to decorate the top). Cut a small cross in the middle, then brush over more beaten egg yolk. Cook in the oven for 30 to 40 minutes, or until golden and puffed up. Serve with steamed greens or **root veg mash** (see page 116), if you like.

FRIED CHICKEN - MY STYLE

TOTAL TIME: 30 MINUTES
PLUS MARINATING

4 higher-welfare skinless, boneless
chicken breasts or thighs

sea salt and freshly ground
black pepper

1 tablespoon smoked paprika

1 teaspoon garlic granules

1 teaspoon ground cumin

1 teaspoon ground coriander

optional: ½ teaspoon chilli powder

3 large free-range eggs

6 heaped tablespoons plain flour

4 heaped tablespoons coarse
ground cornmeal or polenta

6 tablespoons vegetable
or sunflower oil

Slice the chicken into strips, about 2cm thick, then place in a bowl. Add a pinch of salt and pepper and massage in the spices (use the chilli powder if you like a bit of heat, like I do). Cover with clingfilm and leave to marinate in the fridge for at least 30 minutes, though I prefer to leave it overnight.

Beat the eggs and add to the marinated chicken, then mix well to coat. In a separate bowl, mix together the flour and cornmeal or polenta, then season with salt and pepper. Place a large non-stick frying pan over a medium-high heat, pour in the oil and allow to heat up. Coat each piece of chicken in the flour mixture, then add to the pan (you may need to do this in batches) and shallow-fry for 2 to 3 minutes on each side, or until golden and cooked through – be careful as the oil can spatter quite a bit, so make sure the kids stay well away. Remove the chicken to a double layer of kitchen paper to drain, then serve with salad and for an extra special treat, some of my **majestical mac 'n' cheese** (see page 70).

Everyone loves my fried chicken – my friends
say I should open a chicken shop, it's that good!

COD & BUTTERBEAN STEW

SERVES 4

1 medium onion, peeled

2 cloves of garlic, peeled

1 tablespoon olive oil

1 teaspoon smoked paprika

2 sprigs of fresh thyme,
leaves picked

1 red pepper, deseeded

1 fresh red chilli, deseeded

1 x 400g tin of chopped tomatoes

2 x 400g tins of butterbeans

sea salt and freshly ground
black pepper

320g frozen cod fillets
(or any other firm white fish)

1 lemon

Finely slice the onion and garlic, then place in a large frying pan over a medium-high heat with the oil, paprika and thyme leaves. Fry for about 5 minutes, or until soft and jammy, stirring occasionally. Slice the pepper and finely slice the chilli, then add to the pan to fry for another 5 minutes, or until softened. Pour in the chopped tomatoes and butterbeans (including their juice), then season well and let it bubble away for about 30 minutes, or until thickened and reduced.

Turn the heat down to a simmer and add the cod – you want the fish to be submerged in the liquid, so add a splash of water, if needed. Cover with a lid and simmer for around 15 minutes, or until the fish is cooked through, stirring occasionally, but trying not to break up the fillets. Add a good squeeze of lemon juice and serve with extra lemon wedges, basmati rice and a salad, if you like.

This recipe came about by accident one evening when I came home from work, there was no food in the house and my husband, Marlon, was hungry. I threw together whatever I had in stock and this dish was born. It's now one of Marlon's favourites – he loves it with rice, but I prefer mash!

LAMB CHOPS & AUBERGINE SALAD

SERVES
4

TOTAL TIME: 55 MINUTES

2 medium aubergines

3 large ripe tomatoes

2 long fresh green chillies

sea salt and freshly ground
black pepper

1 teaspoon ground cumin

8 x 100g lamb chops

olive oil

1 clove of garlic, peeled and crushed

extra virgin olive oil

optional: a few sprigs of
fresh mint, leaves picked

FOR THE CUCUMBER
& MINT YOGHURT

1 cucumber, peeled

450g thick Greek yoghurt

3 tablespoons dried mint

½ a clove of garlic,
peeled and crushed

TO SERVE

optional: flatbreads

Preheat the grill to high. Pierce the aubergines, tomatoes and chillies, then place under the hot grill for 20 to 25 minutes, or until blackened all over, turning occasionally. Put them into a large bowl, cover with clingfilm and leave to cool.

Meanwhile, make the cucumber and mint yoghurt. Halve the cucumber, scoop out and discard the watery bits in the middle, then finely chop the flesh and place in a bowl. Add the remaining yoghurt ingredients and mix well. Season to how you like it and set aside.

Once the vegetables have almost cooled, mix the cumin with 1 teaspoon each of salt and pepper, then rub all over the lamb chops. Drizzle with olive oil and place in a large non-stick frying pan over a medium heat, then cook for 3 minutes on each side for rare meat, or for longer if you prefer. Transfer to a plate, cover with tin foil and leave to rest for about 6 minutes.

Once the vegetables are cool, scrape off and discard as much of the blistered skin as possible (I leave the chilli seeds in, but deseed if you prefer). Pile it all on a big board, add the garlic, then roughly chop and mix everything together. Season to how you like it, drizzle over a little extra virgin olive oil, then serve with the lamb chops, cucumber and mint yoghurt and with some mint leaves scattered on top, if you like. I love this with a stack of warm flatbreads on the side too. Let everyone help themselves and build up their own wrap, if they want to.

These chops also taste really good with my **Turkish-style couscous salad** (see page 110).

CHEESY POTATO PIE
WITH PIMPED-UP BAKED BEANS

TOTAL TIME: 50 MINUTES

2 x 400g tins of baked beans

1 x **cheesy mash** (see page 116)

100g Cheddar cheese

IF YOU WANT TO PIMP
YOUR BEANS YOU NEED:

1 large onion, peeled

2 cloves of garlic, peeled

2 red peppers, deseeded

1-2 fresh red chillies

olive oil

2 sprigs of fresh thyme,
leaves picked

3 large ripe tomatoes

sea salt and freshly ground
black pepper

Preheat the oven to 220°C/425°F/gas 7. If I'm short of time, I'll keep this simple and empty the beans straight into a sturdy 20cm x 30cm baking tray, so they make a flat layer across the bottom, but, to take it a step further, pimp them up first. Finely slice the onion, garlic, peppers and chilli (I leave the seeds in, but deseed if you prefer). Heat a splash of oil in a large pan over a medium heat, then add the chopped veg and thyme leaves and fry for around 8 minutes, or until softened. Dice the tomatoes and add to the pan for another 5 minutes or so, or until jammy and reduced. Pour in the beans and simmer for a final 5 minutes, then season to how you like it and pour into the baking tray in a flat layer.

Layer the **cheesy mash** on top of the beans, carefully spreading it out to the edges in an even layer, then grate over the cheese (I prefer mature Cheddar, but mild is fine too). Bake for 15 to 20 minutes, or until the beans are hot through, the cheese is melted and golden, and it's bubbling at the edges. Serve with a crisp green salad and homemade coleslaw. This is my fail-safe go-to dish if I'm in need of a bit of naughty comfort food.

These pimped-up beans are also really tasty served in the classic way, on hot buttered toast.

SALMON & PEA RISOTTO

SERVES 4-6

150g frozen peas

1 litre organic vegetable stock

400g fresh or frozen salmon fillets

1 leek, trimmed

2 cloves of garlic, peeled

1 small onion, peeled

1 tablespoon olive oil

3 sprigs of fresh thyme, leaves picked

250g carnaroli or Arborio risotto rice

1 knob of unsalted butter

zest and juice from 1 unwaxed lemon

½ a bunch of fresh flat-leaf parsley, leaves picked

sea salt and freshly ground black pepper

Start by putting the peas (I like petits pois, but any will do) into a colander in the sink and pouring over boiling water to defrost them, then set aside. Pour the stock into a pan over a medium-low heat (I try to use homemade stock, but if you've only got stock cubes, that's fine too). Bring to a simmer, then add the salmon and poach gently for about 12 minutes, or until cooked through (you'll need to up the time by a few minutes if you're using frozen fish).

Meanwhile, finely chop the leek, garlic and onion and place in a heavy-based pan over a medium heat with the oil and thyme leaves. Fry for about 5 minutes, or until softened but not coloured, then add the rice and stir well. Using a slotted spoon, remove the salmon to a plate, then gradually add the stock to the rice pan one ladleful at a time, ensuring that the liquid has been absorbed before adding the next, and stirring constantly. Continue adding the stock for about 20 minutes, or until the rice is cooked through – it should be creamy and oozy, rather than thick and stodgy (you may not need to add all the stock, so use your brain and stop when it's looking good).

Once it's just the right consistency, remove the pan from the heat. Flake in the salmon and add the peas, butter and lemon zest, as well as a good squeeze of juice, to taste. Roughly chop and add the parsley leaves, then stir well. Cover the risotto with a lid and leave to rest for 2 minutes. Stir again, season to how you like it and serve straight away.

SIDES

If you're stuck for ideas, these recipes
will go with just about anything.

TASTY SIDE SALAD

SERVES
10

TOTAL TIME: 15 MINUTES

4 baby gem lettuces, trimmed

1 medium cucumber

4–6 spring onions, trimmed

250g ripe cherry tomatoes

½ a bunch of fresh coriander,
leaves picked

FOR THE DRESSING

juice from 1 lemon

extra virgin olive oil

sea salt and freshly ground
black pepper

Chop the lettuce and cucumber any way you like – this salad doesn't have rules! I like to roughly chop the lettuce into bite-sized chunks and finely slice the cucumber into half-moons, but you might have your own favourite way. Finely slice the spring onions, halve the cherry tomatoes and roughly chop the coriander leaves, then place it all in a large serving bowl and mix gently.

To make the dressing, put the lemon juice and double the amount of oil into a small bowl. Season with salt and pepper, then whisk well. Pour about one-third of the dressing over the salad and toss gently to coat – if it needs a little more dressing, add another drizzle (as long as there's no excess dressing in the bottom of the salad bowl, you're fine). Serve alongside just about anything – I like this with **lasagne** (see page 74) or **fish pie** (see page 76). Store any remaining dressing in a jar in the fridge for up to 3 days.

Don't dress the salad until the very last minute – the acidity from the lemon will make the lettuce lose its crispness, and let's be honest, no one likes a soggy salad.

GRIDDLED COURGETTES
WITH CHILLI, MINT & LEMON

TOTAL TIME: 25 MINUTES

3 large courgettes

½ a bunch of fresh mint,
leaves picked

½–1 fresh red chilli

zest and juice from 1 fat
unwaxed lemon

2 tablespoons extra virgin olive oil

sea salt and freshly ground
black pepper

Trim the tops and bottoms off the courgettes (I like to use a mixture of green and yellow, but just green is fine if that's all you can find), then use a vegetable peeler to peel them lengthways into ribbons.

Place a griddle pan over a high heat (you can use a dry frying pan if you don't have a griddle, but you won't get the nice bar marks). Grab a good handful of the courgette ribbons and put into the pan in a nice even layer, then griddle until nicely charred and bar-marked, turning halfway with tongs (you'll need to do this in batches). Transfer to a covered bowl to keep warm while you griddle the rest (keeping them warm will help the ribbons soak up and take on the flavour from the dressing when you add it).

Finely chop the mint leaves and chilli (I leave the seeds in, but deseed if you prefer), then add to the bowl. Add the lemon zest and juice and the oil, then toss to coat, and season to how you like it. This is great served with grilled fish or meat.

If it's summer, cook this on the barbecue – it'll work brilliantly.

TURKISH-STYLE COUSCOUS SALAD

TOTAL TIME: 15 MINUTES

250g couscous

1 teaspoon ground cumin

1 teaspoon smoked paprika

sea salt and freshly ground
black pepper

1 medium red onion, peeled

1 medium cucumber

2 ripe tomatoes

1 fresh red chilli

1 bunch of fresh mint,
leaves picked

½ a bunch of fresh coriander,
leaves picked

1 bunch of fresh flat-leaf parsley

1 tablespoon tomato purée

2 tablespoons extra virgin olive oil

zest and juice from ½ an
unwaxed lemon

Place the couscous, cumin, paprika and a big pinch of salt into a bowl. Stir to combine, then pour over just enough boiling water to cover the couscous. Cover the bowl and leave for about 10 minutes.

Meanwhile, finely chop the onion, cucumber, tomatoes and chilli (I leave the seeds in, but deseed if you prefer). Finely chop the mint and coriander leaves, and the parsley (including the stalks).

Mix the couscous up with a fork, then stir in the tomato purée until well coated (I do this with my hands – it's messy, but quite therapeutic!). Add all the chopped vegetables, chilli and herbs and mix well. Stir in the oil and the lemon zest and juice, then season to how you like it. Serve as a side with grilled meat or fish or I like it with my **lamb chops & aubergine salad** (see page 98). You can also eat it on its own if you want a light meal or snack.

RASTA MAN VEGGIES

TOTAL TIME: 35 MINUTES

1 medium onion, peeled

3 mixed-colour peppers, deseeded

2 cloves of garlic, peeled

1 fresh red chilli

350g okra, trimmed

100g baby corn

1 large carrot, peeled

100g fine green beans

1 tablespoon olive oil

2 sprigs of fresh thyme, leaves picked

2 large ripe tomatoes

100g mangetout

sea salt and freshly ground black pepper

Start by preparing all your vegetables. Slice the onion and peppers, and finely slice the garlic and chilli (I leave the seeds in, but deseed if you prefer). Cut the okra into 1cm pieces, halve the corn lengthways and slice the carrot into batons about 0.5cm thick. Chop the green beans in half, then set aside.

Heat the oil in a pan over a medium heat, then add the onion, garlic, chilli, peppers and thyme leaves and fry for about 5 minutes, or until softened. Dice the tomatoes and add to the pan, then cook for a further 4 minutes, or until thickened and slightly jammy.

Add all the remaining vegetables including the mangetout to the pan, then stir well. Pour in enough boiling water to just cover (you'll need about 600ml), then lower the heat and simmer for about 10 minutes, or until the sauce is reduced and the vegetables are tender. Season to how you like it and serve with grilled fish or chicken. I also sometimes like this on its own as a nice light lunch.

I invented this dish for my husband, Marlon. It's his favourite way to eat vegetables so I named it after him!

MY FAVOURITE LENTILS

TOTAL TIME: 55 MINUTES

1 small onion, peeled

1 stick of celery, trimmed

1 medium carrot, peeled

½ a bunch of fresh flat-leaf parsley

olive oil

500g dried Puy lentils

1 organic chicken stock cube

3 tablespoons red wine vinegar

2 tablespoons extra virgin olive oil

sea salt and freshly ground white pepper

juice from ½ a lemon

100g feta cheese

Finely chop the onion, celery, carrot and parsley stalks (reserving the leaves for later). Put it all into a medium pan over a medium heat with a drizzle of olive oil and fry for about 5 minutes, or until softened, stirring occasionally.

Stir in the lentils, then crumble in the stock cube and add just enough water to cover (you'll need about 700ml). Bring to the boil, then reduce the heat to low and let it bubble away for 25 to 30 minutes, or until the liquid has reduced by about a half and the lentils are tender, but not mushy.

Leave aside for about 10 minutes to cool slightly, then stir in the vinegar and extra virgin olive oil. Chop and stir in the parsley leaves, then season to how you like it with salt, pepper (I love white pepper, but black is fine here too) and a squeeze of lemon juice, then crumble over the feta. This tastes good either warm or cold, with slow-cooked pork belly, roast lamb, chicken or fish.

If you've got some handy, I sometimes like to fold some sliced, cooked beetroot into my lentils. Delicious!

MASHED POTATO
LOTS OF WAYS

SERVES 4-6

TOTAL TIME: 35 TO 45 MINUTES

FOR BASIC MASH

1.5kg Maris Piper or King Edward
potatoes, peeled

sea salt and freshly ground
black pepper

1 large knob of unsalted butter

100ml semi-skimmed milk

1 whole nutmeg, for grating

Quarter the potatoes, halving any smaller ones, then put into a pan of boiling salted water. Reduce the heat to medium and cook for 10 to 15 minutes, or until tender. Drain in a colander, then return the empty pan to a low heat, place the colander on top and allow the potatoes to steam dry for a couple of minutes. Tip out any excess liquid from the pan, then tip in the potatoes, add the butter and about 75ml of milk. Mash well until light, fluffy and smooth, adding a splash more milk if needed. Stir in a few gratings of nutmeg and season to how you like it. Serve straight away as a classic side or use to top my **fish pie** (see page 76).

For a quick twist on basic mash, there are three different routes I like to go down – at the end, either stir in **2 heaped teaspoons of wholegrain mustard** (delicious with sausages or onion gravy); finely slice and add **1-2 fresh red chillies** for a spicy kick; or to make **cheesy mash**, which I like to use for my **cottage pie** (see page 66) and **cheesy potato pie** (see page 100), simply grate and stir in **50g mature Cheddar cheese**.

Root veg mash is really good with a rich, hearty stew or my **chicken and mushroom pie** (see page 92). Simply follow the basic mash method, swapping out 500g of the potatoes and replacing them with **2 medium carrots and 2 medium parsnips**.

And finally, if you want to go Irish-style, warm **100ml semi-skimmed milk** in a pan over a low heat, then trim, finely slice and add **4 spring onions**. Remove from the heat and allow them to soften for about 5 minutes. Prepare the basic mash recipe, using the infused milk and spring onions, then finely chop **1 small handful of fresh chives** and stir into the mash. This is great with roast pork chops and fried mushrooms.

RICE & PEAS

SERVES
6

TOTAL TIME: 1 HOUR 40 MINUTES
PLUS SOAKING

85g dried red kidney beans

1 spring onion, bashed

1 sprig of fresh thyme

1 clove of garlic, peeled and bashed

5 allspice berries

1 Scotch bonnet chilli, pierced
(see tip below)

½ x 400g tin of light coconut milk

350g basmati rice, rinsed

sea salt

Soak the kidney beans in cold water overnight. The next day, drain the beans and put them into a large non-stick pan over a high heat with the spring onion, thyme, garlic, allspice berries and Scotch bonnet. Pour over 1 litre of boiling water, then cover and bring to the boil. Reduce the heat to medium and simmer for about 40 to 50 minutes, or until the beans are soft.

Fish out and discard the spring onion, thyme, garlic, allspice berries and Scotch bonnet, then pour the cooking water into a large measuring jug, leaving the beans behind. Return 500ml of the hot liquid to the pan, add the coconut milk (save the rest for another time) and bring to the boil, then add the rice and a good pinch of salt. Stir, bring back to the boil, then reduce the heat to low.

Cover the pan with clingfilm and pop the lid on, then leave well alone for 10 minutes, or until the rice is nice and fluffy, and any liquid has been absorbed. Mix it all up with a fork and serve alongside grilled fish or jerk chicken.

My husband is Jamaican and he taught me how to make this dish – we love it in my house and eat it almost every week. Scotch bonnets are really hot, so if you don't think you can handle it, use a fresh red chilli instead.

ROAST POTATOES

SERVES
6

TOTAL TIME: 1 HOUR 20 MINUTES

1.5kg Maris Piper potatoes

sea salt and freshly ground
white pepper

100ml sunflower oil

This is an old family recipe, passed down from my nan – I would never do roasties any other way.

Preheat the oven to 220°C/425°F/gas 7. Peel and quarter the potatoes, halving any smaller ones, then put into a large pan of cold salted water and place over a high heat. Bring to the boil, then reduce the heat to medium and simmer for about 5 minutes, or until just starting to soften and fluff around the edges. Drain in a colander and leave to steam dry.

Meanwhile, pour the oil into a medium non-stick roasting tray and place in the oven to preheat. Return the potatoes to the pan and toss well with the lid on to get them really fluffy around the edges (this is what makes them nice and crispy, so make sure you give them a good shake – don't be too gentle!). Carefully remove the tray from the oven (be careful – the oil will be red hot!), add the potatoes and toss very gently to coat. Season with salt and pepper (I love white pepper, but black is fine here too), then return them to the oven as quickly as possible – if the oil has a chance to cool, you'll end up with greasy potatoes. Roast for 15 to 20 minutes, or until turning golden underneath.

Remove the tray from the oven and spoon out as much oil as you can, then turn the potatoes over and return to the oven. Turn the temperature up as high as it will go and roast for a further 35 to 40 minutes, or until crispy and golden on the outside and light and fluffy in the middle. Serve immediately, with your favourite roast.

HONEY & CUMIN-ROASTED CARROTS

  SERVES 4

6 large carrots, peeled

2 tablespoons runny honey

1 tablespoon olive oil

1 tablespoon cumin seeds

sea salt and freshly ground black pepper

Preheat the oven to 200°C/400°F/gas 6. Cut the carrots lengthways into quarters, then place in a pan of boiling water over a medium heat. Blanch for 5 to 8 minutes, or until tender but still firm. Drain and place in a medium roasting tray, drizzle over the honey and oil, then sprinkle the cumin seeds on top. Toss to coat, then season and spread out in an even layer. Place in the oven for 30 to 35 minutes, or until sticky, golden and caramelized. Serve straight away, with your favourite roast.

Another nice idea for carrots is to roast them with strips of lemon rind and a few fresh thyme sprigs – they'll be less sweet, but zesty and full of flavour.

GARLIC BREAD - THE EASY WAY

SERVES 6

TOTAL TIME: 25 MINUTES

Preheat the oven to 220°C/425°F/gas 7. Pick and roughly chop the leaves from **½ a bunch of fresh flat-leaf parsley**, then peel and crush **4 fat cloves of garlic** and combine with the parsley, **125g of softened unsalted butter** and a good pinch of **sea salt and freshly ground black pepper.** Slice into **1 part-baked ciabatta or part-baked baguette** at 2cm intervals, making sure not to cut right the way through so the loaf stays intact. Spread some garlic butter into each gap, then wrap in tin foil and bake for about 10 minutes, or until the garlic butter has melted and soaked into the bread. Open up the foil and return to the oven for a further 5 to 8 minutes, or until golden. Serve straight away.

GARLIC BREAD - FROM SCRATCH

SERVES 8

TOTAL TIME: 1 HOUR 25 MINUTES, PLUS PROVING

Preheat the oven to 200°C/400°F/gas 6. Grease a 30cm x 40cm baking tray with a little **olive oil** and dust with **plain flour or fine polenta.** Combine and roll out **2 x pizza dough** (see page 52) to roughly the size of the prepared tray, then place in the tray, pushing it out to the edges. Cover with a clean damp tea towel and leave to prove in a warm place for 20 minutes, or until doubled in size. Poke the dough all over to make dimpled pockets. Break up **1 garlic bulb** and bash each clove, leaving the skins on, then poke into the pockets along with **½ a bunch of fresh thyme sprigs.** Drizzle with olive oil and sprinkle generously with **sea salt and freshly ground black pepper.** Bake for 35 to 40 minutes, or until golden and crispy and the garlic is soft. Drizzle over a little **extra virgin olive oil**, then leave to rest for 10 minutes before slicing and serving.

THANK YOU

There are so many people I'd like to thank for making this adventure possible. Firstly, thanks to my wonderful mum, who's always been my biggest supporter, my best friend, my mentor and my teacher. Without her, I wouldn't be the woman I am today – if I'm even half the mother that she is to me, then I know I've done a good job with my own kids. I love you Mum. xxx

Secondly, thanks to my nan and grandad for being the best grandparents in the whole wide world. You are the kindest, most caring, loving people I've ever known, and I love you both from the bottom of my heart. To my gorgeous brother Grant, for being one of my biggest fans since he was born! And thanks to my better half, Marlon, for always supporting me all the way to achieving my dreams – I love you more than words could ever describe.

To the bestest friend I've ever had, Cicek, or as she likes to be called, the Chichmaestro! It seems as though we've been friends for ever – there are so many stories and memories that I'll never forget. There's also nobody I love to cook with more than you – when creating new recipes, you're one of my main inspirations and, of course, you are and always will be my chief taster! I would be completely lost in this world without you. I love you dudey! xxx

To my two other best friends in the world, Caroline and Carly – you guys have had my back from day one, through the good, the bad and the downright ugly! You always keep me in check and are there to guide and support me, no matter what. I love you guys.

I'd like to thank all of my colleagues and the management at my day job at Newpark Nursery for being a great support during the writing of this book, and of course, thanks to all the children for letting me test out my new recipe ideas on them.

A big, huge, massive thank you to Christina Mackenzie, who's done an outstanding job styling my recipes and making them look a million times better than I ever could. I would also like to thank the most amazing photographer I have ever met, the man himself, Mr David Loftus. It was an absolute privilege to have you photograph my book, and I love you!

LOVE YOU ALL!

Thanks to Phillippa Spence, for styling my recipes for my first ever Food Tube videos, which led to me doing this book – you rock! To the rest of the Jamie Oliver team, you've been a constant source of support, guidance and inspiration for as long as I can remember – thank you guys. And Ginny Rolfe – thanks for being the most hard-working, inspirational woman I've ever known, you're amazing and I love you.

Thanks to everyone who has watched and liked my videos on Food Tube – this wouldn't have been possible without you guys. And thanks to all the Food Tube team, including Matt Shaw, Jo Ralling, Emily Taylor, Paul Casey, Ashley Day, Jen Cockburn, and not forgetting the amazing Zoe Collins, who's been there since the very beginning – she was my first interviewer for the Fifteen Apprentice Programme!

I'd also like to give a huge, massive thank you to Rebecca Walker and Malou Herkes for being so supportive and helpful in the writing of this book – I literally couldn't have done it without you guys! xx Thanks also to the lovely designers at Superfantastic, to Penguin, and to Annie Lee and

Pat Rush for copyediting and proofreading this book and doing such a wonderful job.

And last, but by certainly no means least, Jamie Oliver – the big brother I never had. You've always believed in me, even when you probably shouldn't have. You never gave up on me, but instead you've always pushed me to achieve the potential that you saw in me. You've been a constant source of inspiration, knowledge, guidance and motivation, and without you, I wouldn't be where I am today. For that, I'll be forever grateful. Thank you for all the opportunities you've presented me with and for all the experiences we've shared. Most of all, thank you for being my friend. I love you man! xxx

To anybody I may have forgotten, I'm really sorry, but you know what I'm like – love you all!

GOONERS!!!

PENGUIN BOOKS

Published by the Penguin Group

Penguin Books Ltd,
80 Strand,
London WC2R 0RL, England

Penguin Group (USA) Inc.
375 Hudson Street,
New York, New York 10014, USA

Penguin Group (Canada),
90 Eglinton Avenue East, Suite 700,
Toronto, Ontario, Canada M4P 2Y3
(a division of Pearson Penguin Canada Inc.)

Penguin Ireland,
25 St Stephen's Green,
Dublin 2, Ireland
(a division of Penguin Books Ltd)

Penguin Group (Australia),
707 Collins Street,
Melbourne, Victoria 3008, Australia
(a division of Pearson Australia Group Pty Ltd)

Penguin Books India Pvt Ltd,
11 Community Centre,
Panchsheel Park, New Delhi – 110 017, India

Penguin Group (NZ),
67 Apollo Drive,
Rosedale, Auckland 0632, New Zealand
(a division of Pearson New Zealand Ltd)

Penguin Books (South Africa) (Pty) Ltd,
Block D, Rosebank Office Park,
181 Jan Smuts Avenue, Parktown North,
Gauteng 2193, South Africa

Penguin Books Ltd, Registered Offices:
80 Strand, London WC2R 0RL, England

First published 2014

003

Copyright © Kerryann Dunlop, 2014
Photography © Jamie Oliver Enterprises Limited, 2014

Jamie Oliver is a registered trade mark

is registered as copyright
with the Library of Congress
© Jamie Oliver Enterprises, 2013

Jamie Oliver's Food Tube is produced by
Fresh One Productions Limited

Photography by David Loftus

Design by Superfantastic

Printed in Italy
Colour reproduction by Altaimage Ltd

ISBN: 978-0-718-17919-9

www.penguin.co.uk
www.jamieoliver.com
www.youtube.com/jamieoliver
www.freshone.tv

CHECK OUT THE OTHER TITLES IN THIS SERIES: